SHE'S GOT GAME

WOMEN IN BASKETBALL

by A.W. Buckey

FOCUS
READERS®

NAVIGATOR

WWW.FOCUSREADERS.COM

Focus Readers is distributed by North Star Editions:
sales@northstareditions.com | 888-417-0195

Produced for Focus Readers by Red Line Editorial.

Photographs ©: Anthony Nesmith/Cal Sport Media/AP Images, cover, 1; Amy Sancetta/AP Images, 4–5; Ed Zurga/AP Images, 7, 9; Frances Benjamin Johnston/Frances Benjamin Johnston Collection/Library of Congress, 10–11; E. L. Wolven/Library of Congress, 13; Jim Thompson/ZUMA Press/Newscom, 15; AP Images, 16–17; James Mitchell/Ebony Collection/AP Images, 19; Kenneth Lambert/AP Images, 21; Ralph Freso/AP Images, 23; A. Ricardo/Shutterstock Images, 24–25; Zsolt Szigetvary/MTI/AP Images, 27; Dita Alangkara/AP Images, 29

Library of Congress Cataloging-in-Publication Data
Library of Congress Cataloging-in-Publication Data is available on the Library of Congress website.

ISBN
978-1-64493-059-5 (hardcover)
978-1-64493-138-7 (paperback)
978-1-64493-296-4 (ebook pdf)
978-1-64493-217-9 (hosted ebook)

Printed in the United States of America
Mankato, MN
012020

ABOUT THE AUTHOR

A.W. Buckey is a writer and pet-sitter living in Brooklyn, New York.

TABLE OF CONTENTS

CHAPTER 1

UNDEFEATED

On March 29, 1998, nearly 18,000 fans filled an arena in Kansas City, Missouri. They were there to watch a college basketball game. Louisiana Tech's Lady Techsters faced the University of Tennessee's Lady Volunteers. The teams were playing for the college national championship.

Lady Volunteer Chamique Holdsclaw attempts a layup during the 1998 college championship.

The Lady Volunteers had already won the title two years in a row. Tennessee fans cheered, "Three-peat!" They hoped for a third championship. If the Lady Volunteers won, they would become the first women's basketball team to win the title three times in a row.

The Lady Volunteers had already played 38 games during the 1997–98 season. They won every single one of them. And most of their games were not even close. That season, the Lady Volunteers won their games by an average of 30 points.

Tennessee's best player was Chamique Holdsclaw. She was the team's top scorer.

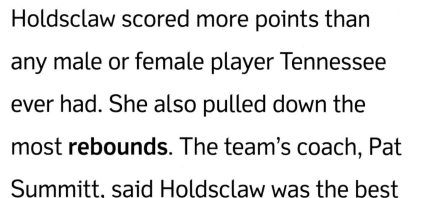

A Tennessee player attempts a basket against a Louisiana defender during the 1998 college championship.

Holdsclaw scored more points than any male or female player Tennessee ever had. She also pulled down the most **rebounds**. The team's coach, Pat Summitt, said Holdsclaw was the best player she had ever seen.

The Lady Techsters played hard. But the Lady Volunteers kept an early lead.

Holdsclaw scored 25 points and grabbed 10 rebounds. The final score was 93–75. The Lady Volunteers stayed undefeated. The team's **perfect season** also involved more wins than any other college team's perfect record, male or female. Best of all, they got their three-peat. It was an amazing season.

PAT SUMMITT

Pat Summitt was a basketball player who then became a coach. She coached the Lady Volunteers for 38 years. Summitt had a tough coaching style. But she cared a lot about her players. As coach, her team won a record-setting 1,098 games. In 2000, Summitt joined the Basketball Hall of Fame.

Tennessee players celebrate after winning the 1998 college championship.

Women have played basketball nearly since the invention of the game. But they have faced obstacles. Some people did not believe women could be good athletes. Others thought women's sports didn't matter. Holdsclaw and the Lady Volunteers helped prove them wrong.

CHAPTER 2

EARLY YEARS

James Naismith invented the game of basketball in 1891. Naismith was a gym teacher in Massachusetts. He wanted a game that students could play indoors. The first basketball players were Naismith's male students. Soon, however, a women's college teacher, Senda Berenson, read about the game.

Female high school students play basketball in 1899.

Berenson brought basketball to her female students in 1892.

Around this time, many people were opposed to women playing sports. Some people believed women were too weak for sports. Others thought that women should get less exercise than men.

BASKETBALL COURT RULES

The first women's basketball courts were split into three zones. Each player was assigned a zone. During a game, players were not allowed to leave their assigned zone. In 1938, women's courts became divided into two halves. But players still had to stay in their assigned zone. In 1971, female players were finally allowed to use the whole court.

Female college students play basketball outside in 1913.

Berenson shared some of these beliefs. But she also thought sports were good for women. As a result, Berenson changed some rules for women's basketball. These rules limited how much women could run and jump during a game.

By the early 1900s, women sometimes could earn money by playing basketball.

For example, Harriet Williams was a basketball player in Iowa. In 1904, her team was paid to play a game for the public. But the town did not have a basketball court to play on. Instead, the game took place on a burned field.

In 1936, two men started a women's basketball team. The team was called the All-American Red Heads. Many players had to dye their hair red. They also performed comedy and tricks. The Red Heads didn't play by traditional women's rules. They played men's teams using men's rules.

The All-American Red Heads traveled to many towns and cities across the

A poster shows off players on the All-American Red Heads in 1971.

United States. They played approximately 200 games a year. Pat Hymel played for the Red Heads in the 1960s and 1970s. She was a comedian and player for the team. By the time Hymel left the Red Heads, women and girls across the United States could play by men's rules.

CHAPTER 3

GOING FOR GOLD

Women have always played a big part in basketball history. But for many years, men had more opportunities to play. In 1972, things changed. The United States passed Title IX. This law requires schools to fund male and female athletes **proportionally**. In 1973, women began to receive college basketball **scholarships**.

Ann Meyers was the first woman to receive an athletic scholarship to a Division I college.

Women's basketball became an Olympic sport in 1976. This addition came 40 years after men's basketball. The Soviet Union won gold that year. The United States won silver. Pat Summitt was a member of the US team. The team's highest scorer was Lusia Harris.

WOODARD THE GLOBETROTTER

In 1984, Lynette Woodard won an Olympic gold medal in basketball. The following year, she became the first woman to join the Harlem Globetrotters. The Globetrotters do not play competitively. Instead, they put on shows during their games. Team members perform a variety of skills and tricks. For example, Globetrotters spin basketballs on their fingertips and do acrobatics while playing.

Lynette Woodard shoots a free throw during a game with the Harlem Globetrotters.

She scored 17 points in a game against Czechoslovakia. Harris was a tall and powerful center. In 1977, the New Orleans Jazz **drafted** Harris to the National Basketball Association (NBA). She was the first and only woman to be officially drafted by an NBA team.

Title IX helped create a new generation of stars. Lisa Leslie was one of them. Born in 1972, Leslie was a basketball star in high school. During one game, she scored 101 points in one half. Leslie continued to excel at the University of Southern California. After college, she helped Team USA win gold in the 1996 Olympics.

In 1997, a new professional league for women arrived. It was called the Women's National Basketball Association (WNBA). Leslie became one of the first WNBA players. She helped the Los Angeles Sparks win back-to-back championships in 2001 and 2002. Leslie made more history in 2002. She became the first

Lisa Leslie dunks during a practice for the 2002 All-Star Game.

woman to **dunk** during a WNBA game. Players like Leslie helped pave the way for many other female basketball players.

DIANA TAURASI

Diana Taurasi was born on June 11, 1982. She played college basketball at the University of Connecticut. Taurasi helped the Connecticut Huskies win three championships in the early 2000s. That was only the second time a women's college team had completed a three-peat.

Taurasi was the first pick in the 2004 WNBA draft. She joined the Phoenix Mercury. Taurasi had great success during her professional career. She helped Phoenix win WNBA championships in 2007, 2009, and 2014. In 2009, she was the league's **MVP**. During her first 14 WNBA seasons, she averaged approximately 20 points per game. And in 2018, she became the first WNBA player to score more than 8,000 career points.

Taurasi has also won four Olympic gold medals. As of 2019, only five people had four gold medals

In 14 seasons (through 2019), Diana Taurasi was an All-Star nine times.

in basketball. No one had five. Many fans agree that Taurasi is one of the greatest women's basketball players of all time.

CHAPTER 4

GLOBETROTTING

Basketball is popular all over the world. More than 75 countries have competitive women's basketball teams. In 2016, 12 of those teams qualified for the Olympics. That year, the US team won its sixth straight gold. In 2018, 16 teams played in the Women's Basketball World Cup. The US team won that event as well.

A French player defends a Brazilian center during a 2016 Olympic game.

As of 2019, the WNBA had 12 teams. However, WNBA players make far less money than NBA players. As a result, many WNBA players play internationally during the WNBA off-season. In 2019, more than half of WNBA players played for a team overseas. Most play in Turkey, Russia, and China. These countries have strong professional women's leagues.

Many US players prefer to play basketball in other countries. From 2013 to 2019, Brittney Griner played for the Phoenix Mercury of the WNBA. She has also played for Russia's UMMC Ekaterinburg. Griner said that Russian women's basketball teams treat players

Brittney Griner dribbles during a 2018 Euroleague game for UMMC Ekaterinburg.

better than US teams do. They also tend to pay players more than US teams do.

In China, basketball is the most popular sport. As of 2019, the Women's Chinese Basketball Association (WCBA) had 18 teams. The WCBA includes many star players. One example is Shao Ting.

Shao has won two championships for Beijing Great Wall, one of the WCBA's top teams.

Shao is a **small forward**. Many have called her the best women's basketball

SHONI SCHIMMEL AND REZBALL

Shoni Schimmel joined the WNBA in 2014. She was an All-Star that year and in 2015. Schimmel grew up on the Umatilla reservation in Oregon. There, she was a star of a basketball style called rezball. The game is played on American Indian reservations across the United States. Rezball players use standard basketball rules. But rezball games are extra fast. Players rarely stop running during a game.

Shao Ting attempts a layup during a 2018 game between China and Korea.

player in China. She played for the Chinese national team in the 2014 World Championship and 2016 Olympics. She was her team's top scorer in both tournaments. In 2017, Shao signed with the Minnesota Lynx of the WNBA. Stars like Shao and Griner show how women keep pushing the game to new heights.

FOCUS ON
WOMEN IN BASKETBALL

Write your answers on a separate piece of paper.

1. Write a paragraph that describes how Title IX affected women's basketball.

2. What do you think can be done to achieve fair and proportional pay between professional female basketball players and male players?

3. In 2002, Lisa Leslie became the first WNBA player to do what?

   A. dunk the basketball
   B. become league MVP
   C. score more than 8,000 points

4. What is the main reason the All-American Red Heads played only against men's basketball teams?

   A. They only knew the rules of men's basketball.
   B. They preferred playing men to playing women.
   C. There were not enough women's teams to play.

Answer key on page 32.

GLOSSARY

drafted
Selected a player in a draft. A draft is a system in which teams acquire new players who are coming into a league.

dunk
To jump into the air and slam the basketball down through the hoop.

MVP
Short for "most valuable player," an award given to a league's best player during a season.

perfect season
A season in which a team never loses a game.

proportionally
Having numbers or amounts that have the same relationship between one another.

rebounds
Plays in which a player controls the ball after a missed shot.

scholarships
Money given to students to pay for education expenses.

small forward
A position in basketball that is usually played by a quick player who is a strong shooter.

TO LEARN MORE

BOOKS

Carothers, Thomas. *Geno Auriemma and the Connecticut Huskies*. Minneapolis: Abdo Publishing, 2019.

Rule, Heather. *College Basketball Underdog Stories*. Minneapolis: Abdo Publishing, 2019.

Scheff, Matt. *Maya Moore: Basketball Star*. Lake Elmo, MN: Focus Readers, 2019.

NOTE TO EDUCATORS

Visit **www.focusreaders.com** to find lesson plans, activities, links, and other resources related to this title.

INDEX

Answer Key: 1. Answers will vary; **2.** Answers will vary; **3.** A; **4.** C